The Wit and Wisdom of
Mothers

This is a STAR FIRE book

STAR FIRE BOOKS
Crabtree Hall, Crabtree Lane
Fulham, London SW6 6TY
United Kingdom

www.star-fire.co.uk

First published 2008

09 11 12 10 08

1 3 5 7 9 10 8 6 4 2

Star Fire is part of The Foundry Creative Media Company Limited

The CIP record for this book is available from the British Library.

ISBN: 978 1 84786 179 5

Printed in China

Thanks to: Cat Emslie, Chelsea Edwards, Andy Frostick,
Gemma Walters and Nick Wells

Images courtesy of: page 4 © Simone van der Berg/Fotolia.com; 7 © iStockphoto.com/Andrew
Dernie; 9 © Dusan Zidar/Fotolia.com; 11 © Eric Threinen/Fotolia.com, 13 © Mazur
Serghei/Fotolia.com, 15 © Stephen Orsillo/Fotolia.com, 17 © iStockphoto.com/Kativ,
19 © iStockphoto.com/Stacy Barnett, 21 © Ivan Piven/Fotolia.com, 23 © kamneed/Fotolia.com,
25 © cynoclub/Fotolia.com, 27 © iStockphoto.com/Misha Shiyanov, 29 © Dale
Trimble/Fotolia.com, 31 © galam/Fotolia.com, 33 © iStockphoto.com/Kent Weakley,
35 © iStockphoto.com/Xavi Arnau, 37 © iStockphoto.com/jclegg, 39 © Stepan Jezek/
Shutterstock.com, 41 © iStockphoto.com/Greg Nicholas, 43 © Aleksandr Lobanov/Fotolia.com,
45 © iStockphoto.com/Dengin Valery, 47 © iStockphoto.com/Cathryn Thomas,
49 © iStockphoto.com/Hanne Melbye-Hansen, 51 © iStockphoto.com/Dave Penn,
53 © iStockphoto.com/Joseph C. Justice Jr., 55 © iStockphoto.com/Bruce MacQueen,
57 © Mike Cavaroc/Fotolia.com, 59 © iStockphoto.com/ Andrew Dean,
61 © iStockphoto.com/johnnyscriv, 63 © iStockphoto.com/Mary Morgan, 65 © Maksym
Gorpenyuk/Shutterstock.com, 67 © iStockphoto.com/Claudia Steininger,
69 © Dhoxax/Shutterstock.com, 71 © Peter Doomen/Shutterstock.com

The Wit and Wisdom of Mothers

Ulysses Brave

STAR FIRE

Foreword

Mothers are the unsung heroes of modern
society. Spending hours of selfless time they
devote their lives to the health and happiness
of their children. Surely it's time to think
about themselves! Packed with common sense
and observation this little book will provide
a treasure trove of such straightforward
advice to mothers of all generations.

Ulysses Brave

Mummy, why is daddy always late?

6

Why is it that even after staying awake all night, wriggling, giggling, yawning and sighing, the children still wake up early?

Why don't you look in
the mirror dear, then you'll be
able to clean it off properly...

Sleeping Tips No. 1:
Grab 40 winks wherever and
whenever you can — you never
know when you'll have to
make do without sleep.

Why is it that fathers are always busy doing something irrelevant when the children need putting to bed?

Learn to distinguish between your children's voices and those other identically sounding children in the playground.

Don't forget that you are the centre of the universe for your children, especially where pocket money is concerned...

Sleeping Tips No. 2:
If they crawl into your
bed, you can be sure that
they will have a better
night's sleep than you.

If you feel like going a little mad, try and do it out of sight of your children and their friends.

It can be lovely when
your children feel
confident enough
to bring their
friends home...

*If your child has forgotten
their favourite blanket, you must
go back otherwise they will
remain rigid with panic.*

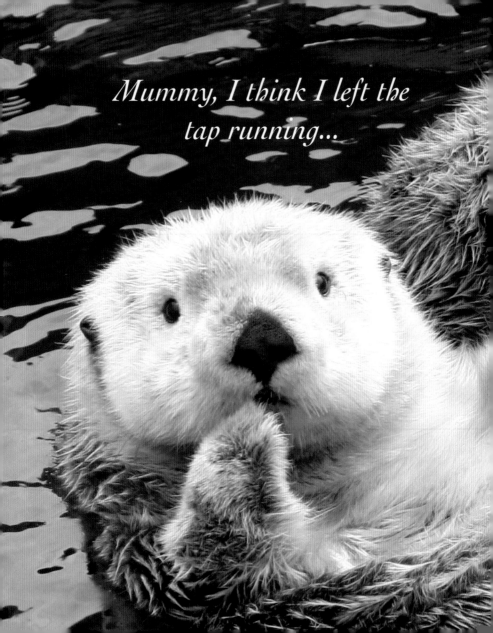

Mummy, I think I left the tap running...

If you are on a diet, try and encourage your children to join in your healthy eating...

Try to encourage your children to jog or go to the gym with you...

If you're feeling fed up,
make sure you have a good
place to hide for a while.

Child psychologists advise that you should not make your children fight you for their food.

*The school run does not have
to turn you into a physical
wreck, but it always does.*

*Hiding from your children
is one of life's guilty pleasures.*

Sometimes you have to eat
what your children eat, just
to get them to eat at all!

A day with your small children and their friends can leave you feeling a little fragile...

Forage for food at every opportunity, your children will thank you when they're older.

Sleeping Tips No. 3:
A lovely dream about Sunday
morning breakfast in bed...

Another serious case of eyes being bigger than the stomach...

Oh yes, I think the tooth fairy will visit again tonight...

It is extraordinary how children and parents seem to synchronise their movements in public...

Always respect your children's whispered secrets, no matter how daft they are.

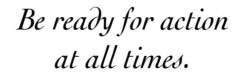

*Be ready for action
at all times.*

If you're feeling peckish at the weary end of the day, try to resist eating the children's food.

If your child bites their tongue, take great interest in the invisible wound.

Practise holding your stomach in before picking up the children in front of all the other perfect mothers...

More secrets, but this time explain that money does not grow on trees.

Motherhood is the endless search for balance and stillness, rarely achieved.

At the end of the day, there's nothing more lovely than a cuddle with your dozing child. Just make sure that the bath is turned off – you'll probably fall asleep too.

Come back soon!